HOW TO
WRITE
MISSIONARY
LETTERS

*Suggestions for writing
effective missionary
prayer letters*

Alvera Mickelsen

MEDIA ASSOCIATES INTERNATIONAL, INC.
Bloomingdale, Illinois
EVANGELICAL MISSIONS INFORMATION SERVICE
Wheaton, Illinois

HOW TO WRITE MISSIONARY LETTERS (Revised. Fourth Edition.)
Copyright © 1988 by Media Associates International, Inc.
First published and copyrighted in 1961 by Evangelical Literature Overseas

All rights reserved.

TO ORDER COPIES OF THIS BOOK WRITE TO:

Media Associates International, Inc.
Box 218
Bloomingdale, IL 60108-0218, USA

Prices at time of printing this book are:

Quantity	Per Copy	Handling and Shipping*
Single copy	$3.50	$1.25
2-5 copies	$3.25	$2.50
6-10 copies	$3.15	$4.00
11-25 copies	$3.00	$5.50
26-50 copies	$2.75	$7.00
51-100 copies	$2.35	$10.00

Prices subject to change without notice.

*Shipments to addresses outside the USA will be sent by surface mail and billed for
overseas postage plus a modest handling charge.

Printed in the United States of America
for Media Associates International, Inc.
Bloomingdale, Illinois, USA
by Weber Graphics Corp.
Chicago, Illinois, USA

CONTENTS

PRAYER LETTER POTENTIAL

Everyone likes to read good missionary letters. Few like to write them. Good writing is difficult; it requires creative thinking and careful planning and this is not easy for most of us.

Yet the potential results of good prayer letters are so tremendous for the future of missionary work that we dare not miss the opportunities we have to share what we are doing.

Expect Results

What are some results of good prayer letters?

• Most important, your missionary **prayer** letters encourage the readers to pray for you, the people among whom you work, and the missionary enterprise as a whole.

• Your letters make known the needs and the opportunities of the work in a particular area and, in turn, enlist consecrated dollars and dedicated workers for missionary service.

• Good letters chart the course of missionary work over time. They address current issues, indicate changes in emphasis, and trace political trends that are significant to missions.

• Good letters help the reader to see that missionaries are intelligent, alert Christians who have a sense of humor and a wholesome attitude toward life.

Attract Attention

If a missionary letter is to fulfill its purpose, it must first be read. "Well," you may be saying, "if I take the trouble to write a letter, those who get it will surely take the trouble to read it." Not necessarily.

Consider for a moment a typical scene. Most American homes are beseiged by "junk mail" that begs to be read. Your letter arrives as part of an average day's stack of three to five form letters. Imagine that the person who opens the mail is a woman. She reads what looks interesting, then dumps the rest into a wastebasket.

What happens to your letter? She takes a quick glance. If it catches her attention, she reads it right away. If your letter is good, she absorbs every line of it and reflects on it for the rest of the day, stopping at times to pray for you as she does her work. She puts it aside to share with her husband and children at dinner or family worship. Over the next few days during her private devotions, she prays for specific items you have mentioned in your letter. The family takes it to prayer meeting on Wednesday night, sharing the prayer requests with others.

Your letter is part of the ongoing written record of missionary work that will inspire and challenge both present and future generations.

Suppose that your letter looks unappealing at first glance. The opening paragraph is dull. The woman's conscience won't let her dump it in the wastebasket with the rest of the "junk mail"; instead, she puts it in a desk drawer to be read when she finds time. The letter lies undisturbed until the drawer is cleaned. A quick look at the date reveals that the letter is old and it is summarily dumped.

The problem is not merely that this letter failed to attract notice; it impressed upon the woman's mind the thought that missionary work is dull and insignificant. That hastily written letter may have saved a few minutes worth of work but may have lost several years worth of support for missions.

What can you do to make sure that your letters will be read from beginning to end? You must **attract** and **keep the reader's attention** through the appearance and the content of your letter.

Appearance is important because it draws attention to the content. Your letter must pass this acid test when the reader is opening the stack of mail to decide what to discard and what to read; it must attract attention. Form letters are easily identified, even with a first class stamp. If the reader is a personal friend, your name alone will attract him or her. Most missionary letters, though, are sent to people who know you only slightly. They'll have to compete for recognition with numerous other letters and magazines.

Your letter must not only **look** but also **be** interesting.

The situation is perhaps comparable to packaging at a grocery store. Suppose you go to the grocery store to buy a can of peaches and discover, side by side on the shelf, two different brands at the same price. One can has a colorful wrapper with a picture of luscious golden peaches on it; the other has a black and white wrapper with only the word "peaches" on it. You would, under normal circumstances, buy the more attractive can. However, if when you ate the peaches you found them tasteless, you would never buy that brand again, regardless of the packaging. You demand quality as well as appearance.

So it is with your letters. Good design and good copy must walk hand in hand. One is never a substitute for the other. The appearance wins attention while the content keeps the reader's interest.

Write Person-to-Person

Think first, second, and always of your reader. Choose a typical reader — maybe an auto mechanic you know in a small town — and write every line with him in mind. One missionary pulls out a card with the name and address of one of his readers and writes with that man or woman in mind. You will naturally avoid many of the common weaknesses of missionary letters if you write with a flesh-and-blood person in mind.

You may wish to refer to the reader in your letter to emphasize that he has a part in your work. One missionary used this technique to interest the reader in literature work:

This morning you mothers got children off to school for the day. No doubt your little ones not old enough for school will spend at least part of their day with their picture books or will come to you with their story books and ask you to read them.

A part of your day will be spent in reading God's Word and gaining spiritual strength for your daily Christian walk.

The newspaper will bring you up to date on the latest developments in Cuba, Algeria, or other areas of unrest in this world of ours.

You may be able to take a few minutes to read more in that missionary biography which is so inspiring or to read a few chapters of fiction which will provide a little time of relaxation.

You will need your Bible for the coming Lord's Day. And so we could go on and on in listing the many books and reading materials available to you each day.

Have you ever thought of what it would be like not to have any books, study helps, the Bible, or other reading material? To not even be able to read or write? This is the plight in which most of our Senufo people find themselves. What a challenge confronts us Ivory Coast missionaries to bring this new world of the printed page to our Africans!

Writing with a person in mind will make you realize the importance of clarity. This sentence says almost nothing to the reader: "One time a group of us visited Killam." Add a few details and the picture becomes clear to the reader: "Yesterday two African evangelists and I bicycled ten miles to Killam, an area where about 300 pygmies live."

"Yesterday Yohan decided to quit work" doesn't tell the reader whether Yohan is male or female, sixteen or sixty, houseboy or evangelist, black or white. How could that reader you are visualizing know these things?

"But," you reply, "I mentioned Yohan in a previous letter." Don't assume that your reader remembers your previous letters. He or she might not have seen the letter that identifies Yohan, or he or she might have read it three months ago. Since that time he or she has read 100,000 words and is enmeshed in problems of work, church, and family. Be sure that everything in your letter can be understood without reference to previous letters.

If when you sit down at the typewriter, you find yourself asking, "What do I feel like writing about today?" then use the following questions as a guide:

"What will be of interest to the reader I have in mind this month?"

"What does he or she need to know to gain a penetrating view of my work?"

"How can I challenge him or her to pray intelligently and consistently for the work over the next few months?"

As you plan and write your letter, remember that you are not addressing a congregation in church; you are talking to an individual in the privacy of his or her own home. You are writing a letter to a person.

2

PRINCIPLES TO PRACTICE

Strong beginnings and memorable endings are two essential principles for good prayer letters. Planning, unity, clarity, and integrity are also important for you to practice.

Plan Ahead

Plan in advance. A good letter requires both spiritual and intellectual preparation. It is rarely achieved by sitting in front of a typewriter and writing whatever thoughts come to mind.

Plan your letter in prayer. Ask the Lord to guide you to the material that will make missions live for your readers. Keep in mind that your letters have a spiritual ministry to your readers. Your letters should prompt them to seek an ever-deepening walk with Jesus Christ.

— Collect information. Make a file with information about the people and area in which you work. Clip articles from newspapers and magazines published in your area. Jot down notes when national leaders make speeches. Maps, geography books, and history books supply facts and figures when you need them.

— Collect interesting letters from other missionaries. They will give you ideas you can adapt for your letters.

— Keep a diary. Scribble bits of description, character sketches or a few significant lines of conversation. You can never retain such details in your mind.

— Keep a record of the letters you have written, so you can see at a glance what subjects you have covered on which dates. Keep copies of all your letters.

Begin at the Beginning

The first sentence in your letter is the most important. It grabs the reader's attention and sets the tone of what is to follow. Work hard on the opening sentence.

You don't need a salutation ("Dear One Who Prays," etc.), but use one if it makes you feel more comfortable.

Avoid easing into your letter with a weak opening, such as "It's been a long time since I've written you, but . . . . ." Introduce the main idea at once. Here are some possibilities:

• Pose a question. One missionary who had just been transferred from Zaire to the Ivory Coast started this way:

"Question: How can you make a new missionary out of an old missionary?"

"Answer: Send her to a new field."

The letter then explained the problems that she faced in starting over as a "new missionary."

Another letter challenged the reader by asking, "What's the sense of praying about a grammar?" It then surveyed what a grammar book would contribute to the literature program as well as the total missionary enterprise.

The opening question in this letter arouses the reader's curiosity:

> How many souls can you buy for two cows? This silly question was very important to a young African Christian not long ago.
>
> The chief of a village 25 miles from the mission station sent word saying he would like an evangelist to come to live in his village. Buba answered the call given in church and said, "I will go." However, he had just planted a large farm with cotton and bought two cows with money he had been saving for years.
>
> Day after day he kept putting off going. His cotton was the best in the district. His cows were healthy and fat. However, any time anyone spoke of it he always said, "I will go soon."
>
> Months went by until one day the elders called Buba in. Again he promised he would go, but he could not bear to leave the best cotton farm and the two fattest cows in the area.
>
> One morning he went to feed his cows and found them both dead! Then and there he told his wife, "God has spoken. Tomorrow we go to preach. Get our things ready." They went the next day.
>
> Four weeks later he came back and reported 15 people had already received Christ. A few months went by and there were 28. Then they

were building a church for the 120 who gathered every Sunday! With a broken heart and tears in his eyes he said, "Had I but gone sooner, the hundreds who died while I waited would also have heard. Now they are in eternity — all because I loved my two cows more than the souls of men!" We often wonder how much the Lord could do if it wasn't for the "cows" in our lives!

• Begin with an anecdote or story. This opening grips the reader's attention with its graphic portrayal of a conversion: "Herroro was drunk, not dead drunk, but in the same kind of stupor he had been in for months or possibly years. Now his heavy blurred voice was saying words which protested against all that he was: 'I want to accept Jesus Christ as my Savior.'"

• Begin with a startling statement. "Today I saw the 'tomb' of Mary, the mother of Jesus — right here in Pakistan," wrote one missionary. The missionary then recounted the teachings of Islam regarding Mary and Jesus.

• Begin with a statement that summarizes the subject of your letter, such as "Islam is awakening the Christian church in Western Europe because of its swift growth."

• Begin with a reference to the reader. One missionary began, "Are you praying extra hard for us this term? It seems so! How else can we explain our deep joy and rich blessings since our return to Argentina? Take, for example, the joy of hearing two young fellows ask, 'Isn't there a village we can evangelize all by ourselves?'"

Here's a good opening for a letter which had an enclosure:

No, no, don't lay that tract down, you must read it, or the rest of this letter won't make sense.
Like it? Here's how an ELWA listener in Tanzania responded. "Your tract sank deep into my heart, in fact it made me to know Jesus Christ as my Savior."
Know why he liked it and came to the Lord? He was familiar with the country fable upon which it was based, and the expressions were African. It was written for him!"

Starting with a Scripture verse is rarely effective. Since the reader will not know its relevance until he finishes the letter, he is apt to skip the verse and start to read below it. Put the Scripture verse in the body of the letter **after** the item to which you want to relate it.

There are countless ways to begin a letter, but whatever one you choose, be sure it reflects the rest of the letter's subject and mood.

Master the Memorable Ending

Prompt the reader to pray for you and your work with a trenchant ending. A 1-2-3 list of prayer and praise items at the end of the letter is often very helpful to the reader, providing you have laid the groundwork in the body of the letter. On the other hand, in many good letters, the subjects for prayer have already been impressed upon the reader and the 1-2-3 list seems superfluous.

When the letter is finished, just stop. Some letters give the impression that the writer is groping for a graceful close. As a result, the letter just "runs down."

Do your readers know for sure **who** you are and **where** you are when they set your letter aside to pray? Always sign both your first and last names. The reader may know three men named "Bill" in Zaire. Don't keep him or her guessing.

Also, put your full address in every letter. You may also help your readers find their bearings by drawing a thumbnail sketch of your country (or continent) and marking an X on your spot. The average reader probably does not know where Mozambique, Sri Lanka, or Morocco is located.

Strive for Unity

Decide the thrust of your letter before you begin to write. A letter that focuses on **one** idea or incident is more forceful. A lack of unity is the most common fault of missionary letters.

There are three principle ways of attaining unity: unity through subject; unity through incident; unity through theme.

To attain unity through subject, isolate a subject and treat it thoroughly. Most readers will welcome the informative, meaty letter that results from limiting yourself to one subject.

Don't be afraid of subjects that are difficult or deep. More letters err by being too shallow than by being too deep. There is a maxim that most writers underestimate the intelligence and overestimate the facts at the disposal of the reader on any particular subject. This is especially true of missionaries. Most readers will grasp the point you are trying to make in your letter if you supply them with all the facts they need.

What kind of subjects should you treat? These are a few possibilities that you can adapt to almost any field:

— the religious beliefs of the people among whom you work

— the problems of raising a family in a foreign culture

— the headaches and the heartaches that accompany each stage of planting a local church in a foreign culture

— the obstacles faced by converts in your area

— the contribution your specialized work (education, medicine, agriculture, radio, literature, etc.) makes to the growth of the church

— the rise of nationalism and its effect on the church

— a case history of a man or woman that describes his or her growth in the Lord

— or, a concise history of missionary work in your area

The list could go on and on.

To attain unity through incident, report a single event in your letter. For example, tell the story of how a church was started, how a family was brought to Christ, or how a national Christian witnessed for Christ through sorrow.

The following example shows the potency of the single-story letter:

> Just a few short years ago a Formosan pastor from the plains wearily toiled up the steep slope of one of the rugged mountains which forms the backbone of this verdant island. Behind him was several hours of trail with almost no respite from the sun. Ahead was a small tribal village perched precariously on a shoulder of the mountain, a village that never had heard the gospel. What would be their response to this strange but wonderful message?
>
> Several hours later his heart was rejoicing over the many who had heard and especially for the one who had believed in Christ. But there was only ONE. Was it worth the long trip? That pastor for some unknown reason never returned, but as the days passed, the Holy Spirit was at work watering the seed.
>
> That one became two, and the two became more as they talked of this new doctrine. Gradually almost the entire village in a very simple way put their trust in Jesus as they met to recall the pastor's words. From somewhere came an old Japanese Bible and a songbook and they grew in the Lord. Smoking and drinking stopped, and the life in the village changed.
>
> Word spread down the mountain to another village in the valley like the flying sparks of a fire touching their hearts. It wasn't long until all but a handful in that village also had believed. After a long day's work in their little mountainside fields they would meet to sing with such volume and simple beauty that it must have made the courts of heaven ring. Several would take turns "talking" about the gospel and reading from the one Bible until the oil lamps burned low.

Then over a year ago a young Taiwanese fellow from Nantow was sent to the village at the foot of the mountain to teach school, but he made his home in the upper village. The people were delighted that someone had come in from the plains and immediately they pleaded, "Tell us some Bible stories."

He didn't know any Bible stories for he had only come in contact with the gospel a few times at our church in Nantow. But he was willing to try. So before he was ever saved he began buying Bibles — reselling them to the younger folk who were soon able to read. Each time he had an opportunity, he walked out to the plains and rode a bus home to Nantow where he listened attentively to the messages so he could go back and repeat what he had heard.

Soon the Lord gripped his heart with his own need and he responded to the One who gives inner peace and happiness. A short while later he was baptized and became a member of the Nantow church. Back in the mountains he joyfully added a spiritual ministry to his long hours of school teaching by adding inspiration to their meetings and to their choir.

Recently Catholic priests have gone into the villages. They said, "We will give you clothes and milk powder, and will also allow you to smoke and drink if you will join the Catholics and start a Catholic church." It was a sore temptation to these folk poor in material things, but they reasoned, "There must be something wrong with a teaching that would let us go back into sin," so the majority stood firm. They invited Ruth Mayo, Felice McKinnon and us to visit them and explain more fully the Scriptures regarding this.

So we, armed with a shovel and pick to get over the rugged logging road, and with flannelgraph and slides for the folk to see, bounced in as far as the car could possibly go, walked across a long, rickety suspension bridge that should have fallen in years ago, and climbed the steep trail toward the village. The folks met us with a royal welcome and carried everything, even our Bibles, for us.

When we arrived at the cluster of mud brick and wooden houses with their straw, slate or hand-made shingle roofs, we were met by a crowd who shook our hands and greeted us with "Peace." We were dumbfounded — where had they learned to shake hands? It isn't a prevalent habit down on the plains. Every one that was big enough to walk had to shake hands with each one of us, and even the shy ones made a quick grab and then let go.

They gave us the best they had as they took us into one of the better houses. The furniture was comprised of a table and four benches. Some old snapshots were hanging and the board walls papered with old newspapers. Chickens and mangy dogs wandered in and out over the mud floors.

Somewhere the villagers got hold of an old Japanese generator and they were in the process of putting lights in all the houses. Each house was allowed one 15-watt bulb on a long cord which could be carried from the kitchen to the main room as needed. At night it gave just enough light to see vaguely what we were eating.

The village was one of the more fortunate ones for they had a stream of water nearby, but they weren't too adept at using it in keeping clean.

It was about 9:00 that night when they pounded the iron bar gong and everyone packed into the little rough-hewn church. They sang the old plaintive mountain tunes with Christian words, four-part harmony, new choruses and even a quickly learned, "Hallelujah, hallelujah, Praise ye the Lord," in English as Stan taught them. Their lusty, melodious singing would put to shame you folks at home. Then we had flannel-graph, slides and messages. It was near midnight before anyone wanted to go home.

The next morning Stan spent about four hours with a little group answering Bible questions and searching out important Bible teachings. Then as we prepared to go back down the mountain again we had to run the gauntlet of hundreds of handshakers and well-wishers.

Returning home we were itchily aware that we were taking something from the village with us. A couple of us were covered from head to feet with flea bites before we finally got rid of the pests. But the blessings of rich fellowship and seeing what the Lord had done was worth all the misery of scratching during the following days.

Praise the Lord for His wondrous works! And pray that these folk will grow stronger and continue to resist the forces of evil which would seek to destroy the unity and faith they now have.

To attain unity through theme, choose one dominant idea and develop it through a number of instances. Through the theme of "heartbeat" the letter of a nurse forged a line between medicine and evangelism:

This morning, like every Saturday morning, after the hospital work was under control, I slipped into the "zala" (delivery) room to examine expectant mothers. The stethoscope amazes them, for they probably can't understand how I can listen and learn about something I can't see.

It took us so very much longer today because I endeavored to ask all my routine questions in Kinyuranda. Another language, you ask. Yes, another language, and when I use the stethoscope and listen for heartbeats of little Zaire-folk-to-be, I realize that I must conquer the tribal language if I ever want to know the heartbeat of these Wanyuranda folk.

At the beginning of the new year, I made a vow that I would conquer one lesson a week for the coming year. This week finds me still on the fourth lesson! Why? The wards have been full with little kiddies these days as an epidemic of measles has swept through the Bible school village and Chrstian village. We haven't lost a life yet, thanks to the doctor's good medicine and God's watchcare over them.

Pray that the Lord shall make the desire to win these folk so strong and my burden for their hearts so practical that it will be a JOY to sit down in my spare minutes and tackle this language. I want to HEAR the heartbeat of Zaire women!

Yesterday at 5:00 p.m. was the "treat" hour of the week as I sat in with 18 students studying personal evangelism. It took me back to Bible school days when it was so wonderful to have the Word opened, taught, and applied.

It seems just as wonderful now to sit before one of His Zaire servants and allow the Holy Spirit to show us by His Word — through the lips of Musa, our teacher — our task here in Zaire land! Student nurses and missionary Trudy alike were needing this "refresher" course.

Musa described the experience of the woman at the well and how she left her water pots. (She couldn't have run as fast if she hadn't.) At the end of the class he asked how many had talked to one person about his or her soul this week. (Three out of the 19 had!) I couldn't help but say, "thank you, Lord, for this class."

Pray that the Word shall become a sharp and ready tool for nurses and missionaries together to win the heartbeat of these Zaire sick folk for Jesus Christ!

One afternoon last week, I looked down into my garden and saw four goats "going to town" on my sweet potatoes. I started down the hill with the usual "chip on the shoulder" attitude we have when we deal with native animals in white folk's gardens. Paulo, a student nurse, was trying to chase them away and when I asked him who they belonged to he answered, "I don't know."

He tied them up in a poli patch nearby and came back and said, "Mademoiselle, those are my goats. I was afraid to tell you at first."

I went home and thought of my outward anger and of Paulo's lie; then I wrote a forgiveness letter.

In a few days, Paulo replied:

"Mademoiselle Trudy — Many greetings in our Lord Jesus Christ! I received your letter and thank you very much, but I also remained to think very much about the things that you said to me and I began to see sin in my own eyes. Thank you for forgiving me and I have finished to forgive you. Matt. 6:14,15. Thank you for your letter. It helped my heart very much. You are our "mamma teacher" and a mother has permission to correct her child when he does bad, therefore it wasn't necessary for me to forgive you."

Note how the following letter centers around the "Learners" theme:

One day in Minneapolis, Dr. R. E. Thompson, veteran missionary from China, told us, "during your first term remember you are always walking around with a big letter L on you. That L signifies LEARNER. You will be nothing but a LEARNER through your entire first term." How true those words have been! How often we have reminded each other that we are still only LEARNERS.

We've been LEARNING what it feels like to be a foreigner —to live in a strange land amidst a strange people who speak a strange language and have such strange customs. We wonder why everyone insists on eating supper at 9:00 p.m. Ridiculous! And only a piece of bread and a cup of coffee for breakfast. And why do they clap their hands at the front gate instead of knocking on the door? Or why does Carlos come and chat endlessly before telling us he wants to borrow the bike? Why doesn't he ever get to the point and be frank like the Americans? And why are folks so easily offended when we say we haven't time to stay? When will we LEARN that we MUST stay and visit an hour, or it's better to not go at all?

The Latins are polite people and we must LEARN to be the same — to always greet the meatman, the storekeeper, the postman and ask how the family is before making our purchase. We must adjust to these people and their ways because this is their country. We are the foreigners.

We're LEARNING other things too. The Spanish language is beautiful when spoken properly, but our faulty pronunciation, limited vocabulary, groping for words, wrong use of verb forms cause us much embarrassment. If we are to ever dominate this language, we need to converse more, read more, think more, live more in Spanish. It's a task to LEARN a new language.

Unity should not be confused with uniformity; thus, aim for variety in the type of letters you write. While you should put to good use your talent for a certain type of letter, you will give a more interesting and complete picture of your work if you vary the handling of your letters from time to time.

Don't depend on feeling or intuition for this. Prepare a chart of the type of letters you have written for the past several months or years. Then resolve to fill in the gaps by writing about topics which you have consistently omitted.

Be Dramatic

Drama is produced when your letter strikes a balance between showing and telling the reader what happened. This letter shows a linguistic team in action, then offers an explanation:

Dear Friend,
    If you were to eavesdrop at our door these days, you might hear something like this:
    "Mo fungi nying" (cool off your insides) . . . That would be Sagbana

telling our informant not to get excited and not to talk so fast while we are trying to write down his words.
"Have him say that again with the negative word after it. I want to see if that verb has all low tones or if it comes up to a midtone on the end." That would be I; and I am not always sure of the tones I hear unless I can hear them next to a word whose tone I already know.
"Did you hear the down-glide on that tone and how long he made the vowel? I suspect that's just a contraction of their midtone pronoun and the low-tone indicator which tells you the verb is in the future." That would be Betty Mills; her ears seem to be the sharpest when it comes to hearing tone changes, and often just a change in tone will give us a clue that helps us understand some grammatical construction.
"I want to play some of this back on the tape to see if this man's voice is recording clearly and loudly enough." That would be Dick Mills; he is the one who runs the tape recorder and elicits from our various informants how they say things in their particular dialects.
This is our "team" at work getting material to make a comparison of all the important language dialects on our field. Dick and Betty have selected 23 pages of words and sentences which cover the main grammatical constructions as well as all the possible tone patterns on nouns and verbs in our dialect. Now we are working to get these same words and sentences from each of the other dialects. When we have finished, we will have some basis of determining likenesses and differences in each. This, in turn, will help us know which dialects can be reached with the same translation of the Scriptures, with the same literacy materials, by a missionary speaking another dialect, etc.
Dick goes out and brings back an informant to the station. There he records all the material on tape, and at the same time Betty and I write it down on paper. Often we use three languages in the process (four, counting the comments among ourselves in English as we try to figure out what we are hearing). Dick gives a word in French to Sagbana; Sagbana says it in the Dyoula (jewel-ah) trade lanaguage to the informant, who in turn repeats it in his own dialect.
We have already recorded material from our Korhogo, Nielle, and Ferkessedougou stations. This week and next we are visiting in Boundiali, working with the missionaries here as we record a number of dialects in this area. We expect to go to Dabakala for a week at the end of the month. Dick also has four dialects on tape which we weren't able to write down at the time he recorded them, so they all must be gone over and written down. PRAY for physical strength for each of us (eight hours a day listening and concentrating can be very fatiguing!). Continue to PRAY that Sagbana will yield his heart completely to the Lord.
Three years ago today I sailed from New York on the Queen Mary. How I praise the Lord for His continual faithfulness and for every experience He has brought into my life! Thank you, too, for your gifts and prayers which have made it possible for me to serve the Lord here.

Dramatic stories are not always available. But often missionaries fail to see the essential drama around them.

One missionary wrote a thrilling account of a mule trip in the Andes Mountains. The missionary who accompanied him on the trip later said, "I got more excited when I read Jerry's account of the trip than I did on the trip itself." The writer did not exaggerate or dress up the facts; he simply sensed what was truly dramatic about what seemed prosaic at the time.

Develop a keen sense of **sight, sense, sound, taste,** and **touch** when you write. This allows the reader to enter more fully into the experience.

Use dialogue whenever possible. Few things spark up a letter (or any written material) as well as several lines of good dialogue. Incidentally, good dialogue is a condensed version of what people actually say and the way they say it. Don't be afraid to condense five minutes of actual talk into five lines.

Note how dialogue improves this letter:

"And what can I do?" That question! At times it has caused my ire to rise and other times I have felt defeated by it. So often it is used as an answer, and in many ways it describes the outlook of the people. For instance: at girls' camp in Chikalda we had a shortage of water. To keep the girls from wasting water, we placed a woman by the washroom door. Suddenly I heard what seemed to be gallons of water rushing away. Upon going to see, I found the woman yelling and screaming at the girls — little girls, not big ones — telling them not to use so much water. The three girls had each used two buckets and were now ready to use the third. I said to the woman, "Why do you think we put you here?"

"The girls won't listen to me and what can I do?" she answered.

"Haven't you got two hands? Can't you take hold of the buckets and stop them?" I asked.

"But they won't listen to me. What can I do? What can I do?!" she replied.

It seemed that no matter how many different things I told her she could do, she kept repeating, "What can I do?" It was exasperating.

This was only a small thing, BUT this very idea carries over into every phase of life. In the hospital the child won't take the medicine so the parents say, "The child says, 'No,' so what can we do?"

If it is only a matter of a few days' teaching, it remains a small thing, but it goes further. We had a six-year-old child in the hospital severely burned on the back; therefore, we kept him lying on his stomach. Oh, how that child cried to lie on his back! So the parents put him on his back. I asked them, "Why have you done this?"

"He cried to lie on his back and what could we do?" they answered. Day be day we had to watch carefully that the parents didn't turn him on his back.

After we put the heat cradle on and did away with all the dressings, the mother kept saying, "Put dressings on the burns, put dressings on the burns." We showed her how much better the child was getting, explaining how this was the best treatment. She wouldn't have it. Finally the father came to me saying, "How much is our bill? We are going home." I was surprised and asked why. "The mother can't stand to see the burns not dressed. She says to go home. And what can I do?" he said.

Looking at him I answered, "Brother, you're the head of the house. You can say, "Stay here,' and they'll stay. If you take that child home, he'll die. If he dies it will be your fault. What kind of love is this?"

"Oh, no, if the child dies, it will be his fate. The mother can't stand the undressed burns and says 'go home.' And what can I do?" he replied.

Even after much persuasion they still insisted on signing the child out of the hospital. Later he died. When they brought me the news, they said, "It was his fate; that's why he died. And what could we do?"

Many carry this same question over into the spiritual realm. How many, many times after explaining the way of salvation so clearly have I been faced with the question, "It's all in God's hands. What can we do?"

"No, it is in YOUR hands. God has done everything. God sent His Son Jesus. Jesus has died and rose again for you. You have to choose. Will you go to heaven or hell?" I've answered.

"God knows. Whatever our fate is, that it will be. What can we do?" The fatalistic question says nothing — absolutely nothing —can be done. Whatever fate is, that it is. Oh, that I might get across to the people that there *is* something they can do.

Don't write sermons, not even short ones. Your readers hear lots of sermons. They read devotional books. You have something which you can give them — news of the Lord's work in your particular area.

At Christmas, Easter, and Thanksgiving many missionaries replace their regular letter with a short seasonal meditation or poem. It may seem like the easy way out, but resist the temptation. Your sermons are less likely to be read at Christmas than at any other time. Most people barely have time to open Christmas cards and observe the name on the bottom, much less to read "sermonettes"; but they will read a letter that with a few deft strokes depicts how people in another part of the world observe Christmas.

Be Clear

Don't worry about being clever or developing a literary style. Do worry about being clear and making sure the reader easily and fully understands what you are saying. Above all, don't use pious phraseology in the effort to "sound like a missionary." Do use the kind of language which comes naturally to you.

Translate all terminology which may not be understood by all your readers. In many countries, distance is measured in kilometers instead of miles; but the average American has no idea how far 50 kilometers is. Translate it into miles. Likewise, the values of foreign currencies — francs, pesos, rupees, etc. — are second nature to you; they are not to your reader. Many other terms — such as mela, catechumen, bwana, or gendarme — that constantly appear in missionary letters require an explanation or a substitution.

Identify people and places. "Ben Olson, our field director," or "Olufemi Oni, our national pastor," facilitates understanding. "Ibadan, the capital of Nigeria," cues in the reader to geography. Lest you think the reader ought to know such things, ask yourself how many capital cities you know on a continent other than the one in which you work.

Be specific. Avoid vague statements, such as "Pray for a very real need we face at present," or "I'm much stronger after my long illness." Such euphemisms are maddening to the reader. They make him feel left out, as though you were writing to someone else who knows the answers to "what need?" and "what illness?" Either say more or don't say anything at all.

Aim for simple, uncluttered sentences. The subject-predicate order is the easiest to read and to understand. Beware of sentences that only make sense when you reach the end.

A sentence that requires unnecessary backtracking is awkward: "Because of the disillusionment and sense of bewilderment which followed the war, the Japanese people, for a period, listened eagerly to the gospel." This sentence is much easier to comprehend when it is shortened and every part of it made to move forward: "The Japanese people were disillusioned and bewildered after the war. During this post-war period, they listened eagerly to the gospel."

Any sentence that exceeds 30 words demands scrutiny; it would likely benefit from being divided in two. Most sentences in missionary letters are too long and contain too many ideas. A single sentence should not constitute a whole long paragraph. While a succession of short (10- to 12-word) sentences makes letters choppy, few err in that direction.

Short paragraphs are usually easier to read than long paragraphs. They also make a letter look more interesting.

Rambling accounts of day-to-day activities are better suited to a diary than to a missionary letter. An appalling number of letters seem composed primarily of "last week we had a meeting in village A with 20 people there; then we drove home and got a night's sleep and the next day we visited the out schools around village B and that night we had a meeting in village C . . ." and on and on and on. An annual summary of the number of meetings held, or patients treated, or villages visited may be in order.

Check your letter for grammatical correctness. (If you are unsure of the rules of grammar, ask someone to help you.) Use a dictionary regularly. Misspelled words leap from the page and stay longer in the minds of some readers than the content of the letter. Furthermore, such errors make you look illiterate to sharp high school and college students who should be challenged for missionary work. Subconsciously they may think that missionary work is for the not-so-bright people.

Revise and rewrite your letter at least once. Professional writers habitually rewrite two or more times. After your first draft is finished, lay it aside for a day. When you pick it up again, imagine that you are a mechanic in a small town and read it through his eyes. You'll see the sentences which are not clear, which give a wrong impression, or supply irrelevant material.

Maintain Integrity

Integrity means wholeness and honesty. Assume for our purposes that your letters are the only contact the readers have with missions. Are they getting a fair, comprehensive, well-balanced picture of missionary work — the plans, the disappointments, the victories, and the future possibilities?

Show both the forest and the trees. Keep the readers in touch with your family and its progress, but don't let the family dominate your letters. Write about how communism, Buddhism, nationalism, or Islam threaten or impede missionary work in your area, but don't make all your letters historical or sociological treatises.

Be generous with stories about the people among whom you work. Let readers see them as people with the same feelings and sorrows and joys that they experience. Only then are your readers truly compelled to pray for them.

The poignant plea for prayer in this letter about money is effective largely because of the insight it gives into individual lives:

> One of the biggest problems which a missionary faces on the field is MONEY. Please don't misunderstand me in thinking that I mean the lack of it, or that this is a plea for money. It is not. My experience has been that the Lord provides according to our needs (not our desires, necessarily). But the problem lies in the faithful administration of funds entrusted to us.
>
> What would you do:
>
>> If two out of three daughters eligible for girls' camp could not attend because the parents did not have sufficient money to pay the travel expenses of them all;
>>
>> If your workers did not keep accurate accounts of monies entrusted to

them and handed in exorbitant requests for reimbursement;

If a talented young man desiring to be a medical doctor in a Christian hospital lacked funds for his education partly because his father was in the Lord's work;

If your workers suffered a sudden loss of money and possessions because they were caught in mob rioting while traveling to your station, even though the loss to two of the families could have been avoided if they had followed your instructions;

If part of the money your workers had lost was money they had borrowed and were responsible to return;

If because in their eyes you are rich, you face the constant begging of people you want to have as friends.

Please pray that I may have wisdom from the Lord in dealing with money problems, that I may have a sympathetic understanding of the real needs, that I may be able to deal with each individually with kindness and love, that I may be able to point people to God who can supply all their needs rather than draw them to myself, and that I may be able to win their love and respect even though I may refuse some of their requests.

Treat nationals with respect and sympathy in your letters. One missionary said he never wrote anything in his letters that he wouldn't be willing to have the nationals read. It is important that your letters help the reader to look at problems from the national's vantage-point.

Missionaries **can** exert influence on the perceptions of the public (at least the Christian element) by exercising responsible leadership. Many members of the public think that the American cultural brand of Christianity is the fountainhead of wisdom and the dispenser of all that is good. It's high time they learn better. You can cater to the readers' petty provincialisms, or you can bring them up-to-date on current events in the church at large.

Make use of humor when possible. One of the basic rules of psychology is that people turn away from what is unpleasant. Humor not only lightens but balances the load your letter is carrying. Missionary work is difficult, but it is not grim.

Funny, sympathetic stories about the people with whom you work are fine if they don't belittle. Even better are stories that make **you** the butt of the joke. Your life is full of funny things — language errors, misunderstandings about the culture in which you live, and so forth. When readers see that you are able to laugh at **yourself,** they'll like you better, and the deeper their affection for you, the more natural it becomes for them to pray for you.

Be honest about your feelings and reactions in your letters. This missionary's candor is refreshing: "Returning home we were itchily aware that we were taking something from the village with us. A couple of us were covered from head to feet with flea bites before we finally got rid of the pests. But the blessings of rich fellowship and seeing what the Lord had done was worth all the misery of scratching during the following days!"

Don't paint glowing portraits of work that doesn't really glow. Highlight the victories whenever you can, but don't hesitate to reveal the discouragements, the hard problems, and the defeats. Give an accurate, well-balanced picture of your work.

3

PICTURE YOUR LETTER ON PAPER

You can often greatly improve the appearance of your letter without additional expense or undue labor. After you've written the first draft, sketch a rough layout. Rewrite your letter carefully and set it up on the typewriter, leaving room for illustrations, headings, and so forth. Keep in mind the following pointers:

Keep It Simple

The appearance of the letter should enhance rather than detract from its content. If an intricate or unusual design makes your letter hard to read, skip it. Restrict handwritten copy to signatures; it is often indecipherable when mimeographed or xeroxed.

Don't crowd your letter. Plan to leave a space between paragraphs and to have generous margins on all four sides. An absolute minimum for margins is one inch.

Decide the length of your letter in advance. Don't let it spill onto the next page because it happens to be a few lines too long; a few lines can always be cut. Most missionaries who write frequently cover only one side of a single page. Some subjects, however, cannot be handled adequately on a single page. If you are sure the subject merits more than one page, write the second or third page with a clear conscience.

Use the Resources at Hand

The basic instrument by which missionary letters are set up — whether they are mimeographed, or xeroxed, or printed by the offset process —is the typewriter. Experiment with the full range of devices on your typewriter. Delineate boxes or columns with asterisks, hyphens, or colons for added emphasis and appeal.

Use colored paper, colored ink, or both. Any one of the brilliant array of colored papers costs little more than white paper. The same is true for colored inks, although changing the ink on a mimeograph machine can be a time-consuming and messy business. Stick to the dark tones when you use colored ink: dark brown, purple, navy blue, dark green, etc.

Enliven your letters with hand drawings. A natural choice of illustration is stick figures, although success depends on drawing pictures that are animated and detailed:

THE FIRST DELIVERY IS HISTORY: Native women have been coming to the dispensary for pre-natal care, and one reported as usual that morning. Then about noon the Wood-cutter called Peg saying that a woman was dying out in the brush.

Peg went out to find the woman sitting in the weeds about 20 yards behind the dispensary, holding her new-born baby.

She had followed the native custom and delivered her baby in the "poli" even though she had been to the dispensary so many times. When she and the baby were cared for, the mother took her precious prize, wearing a new shirt and wrapped in a soft blanket, and walked home, possibly several miles.

THIS, TOO, IS MISSIONARY LABOR: We kept track of our guests for one month and were interested to find that we (that is, Bothwells and Penneys as a station) entertained 92 overnight guests and served 208 guest meals. Wouldn't you all like to drop in? No, we are not running a hotel, but members of our own CBFMS family and others find it necessary to come as they enter Zaire, leave on furlough via Bukavu, or come because of business. Our thatched guest house is an attempt to give the visitors a place to stay while we try to carry on the regular work with as little interruption as possible.

LANGUAGE SCHOOL NO. 2: On October 17, Marie Bothwell, teaching all morning classes, and Don, in charge of the afternoon informal hour for each pupil, will begin to teach eight new missionaries their first African language. There will be two families in each house (even the "guest house") with a small nursery of 10 kids. Eleven mouths will be at each of two tables.

If you cannot do even the simplest drawings yourself, invest in a book of drawings which can be copied in your letters. Start your own file, too, of clippings from national newspapers and magazines. Trace simple outlines from the pictures and use them in your letters to portray what life is like in the country where you serve. (You will not violate any copyright laws in so doing.)

If the drawings you find in books or your own file do not exactly fit, you may alter them slightly to suit your purposes. One missionary drew caricatures of himself by adding a pair of glasses and a shock of unruly hair to the pictures he traced from various sources.

Put photographs in your letters often if you are using the offset process. The impact of a letter with photographs is worth the slight difference in price. Steer clear of the photograph in which a group of people stares into the camera; it lacks both informative and emotive value. Sharp, dramatic shots that capture **someone doing something** are welcome.

Be sure the picture is in focus and has good contrast. Most pictures lose some detail in the printing process, so a fuzzy, gray one will look even worse when reproduced.

Add Variety

Vary the form of your letter. Arrange paragraphs in new patterns or cast headings in capital letters or in bold-face type. An unusual approach to form in the following letter invites the reader's participation:

QUIZ YOURSELF

We sometimes get questionnaires from people who are interested in our work, so we thought we would reverse things and let you quiz yourself about missions in French West Africa. Here we go:

1. CHECK WHICH OF THE FOLLOWING IS A PART OF A MISSIONARY'S WORK
   ☐ Building a house.
   ☐ Learning the language.
   ☐ Transporting sick people to dispensaries or hospitals.
   ☐ Translating Scriptures and other literature.
   ☐ Answering letters.
   ☐ Keeping house.
   ☐ Killing snakes, scorpions, spiders, etc.
2. TRUE-FALSE
   ☐ Missionaries are "super-human" and can do no wrong.
   ☐ Pills and prayer are equally vital in his daily life.
   ☐ Missionaries are never discouraged.
   ☐ A letter from YOU could bring encouragement to a missionary.
   ☐ Children of missionaries in F.W.A. must attend school far from

their parents eight months of each year for the sake of their
health.
3. MULTIPLE CHOICE
   □ Pagan Africans most need: clothing, food, Christ.
   □ African languages are: easily learned, impossible to learn, learnable
     but very difficult.
   □ Most of the Africans in the northern Ivory Coast have often, never,
     seldom heard the gospel story.
   □ Every Christian should see to it that his pastor, the head deacon, he
     himself prays more for the spreading of the Word.
4. STATE IN 25 WORDS (OR MORE):
   "My part in telling the gospel in F.W.A. is _____
   _____
   _____

If you checked all of Part 1, you're so right! This is only a partial
list.
   I think the True-False are quite obvious, but perhaps we need to be re-
reminded of these things.
   Part 3 is there to remind you of our Africans who need Christ. Most of
them have never heard of Him and their language is very difficult, but
learnable.
   You ask the Lord to check your answer to Part 4.
   I hope you made a good score. Perhaps you can use the quiz this month
as an outline as you pray for us and the Lord's work in the Ivory
Coast.

Indenting paragraphs by an odd number of spaces makes each of them
stand out:

One of the biggest problems a missionary faces on the field is MONEY.
Please don't misunderstand me in thinking that I mean the lack of it, or
that this is a plea for money. It is not. My experience has been that the
Lord provides according to our needs (not our desires, necessarily). But
the problem lies in the faithful administration of funds entrusted to
us.
   What would you do:
If two out of three daughters eligible for girls' camp could not attend,
because the parents did not have sufficient money to pay the travel
expenses of them all;
      If your workers did not keep accurate accounts of monies
      entrusted to them and handed in exorbitant requests for reim-
      bursements;
            If a talented young man desiring to be a medical doctor in a
            Christian hospital lacked funds for his education because his
            father was in the Lord's work;

If your workers suffered a sudden loss of money and possessions because they were caught in mob rioting while traveling to your station even though the loss of two of the families could have been avoided if they had followed your instructions;
>If part of the money your workers had lost was money they had borrowed and were responsible to return;
>>If, because in their eyes you are rich, you face the constant begging of people you want to have as friends.

Please pray that I may have wisdom from the Lord in dealing with money problems, that I may have a sympathetic understanding of the real needs, that I may be able to deal with each individually with kindness and love, that I may be able to point people to God who can supply all their needs rather than draw them to myself, and that I may be able to win their love and respect even though I may refuse some of their requests.

An alternate way is to indent important paragraphs on both the right and the left sides:

Dear Friend,
One of the problems a missionary faces on the field is MONEY. Please don't misunderstand me in thinking that I mean the lack of it, or that this is a plea for money. It is not. My experience has been that the Lord provides according to our needs (not our desires, necessarily). But the problem lies in the faithful administration of funds entrusted to us.

What would you do:
>If two out of three daughters eligible for girls' camp could not attend, because the parents did not have sufficient money to pay the travel expenses of them all;
>If your workers did not keep accurate accounts of money entrusted to them and handed in exorbitant requests for reimbursements;
>If a talented young man desiring to be a medical doctor in a Christian hospital lacked funds for his education because his father was in the Lord's work;
>If your workers suffered a sudden loss of money and possessions because they were caught in mob rioting while traveling to your station even though the loss of two of the families could have been avoided if they had followed your instructions;
>If part of the money your workers had lost was money they had borrowed and were responsible to return;
>If, because in their eyes you are rich, you face the constant begging of people you want to have as friends.

Please pray that I may have wisdom from the Lord in dealing with money problems, that I may have a sympathetic understanding of the real needs, that I may be able to deal with each individually with kindness and love, that I may be able to point people to God who can supply all their needs rather than draw them to myself, and that I may be able to win their love and respect even though I may refuse some of their requests.

Sincerely in Christ,

The poetic form of this letter makes the words leap out at the reader:

Dear Friends:
It makes a difference where you are. Today sub-zero weather in these northern states brings out:
Heavier clothing, warm gloves and boots.
The scraping sound of snow shovels,
The smell of applied remedies for colds and coughs,
The hurry to the service station for anti-freeze for your car,
because it's mid-winter in this part of their country.
But, if you were in Quepe, Chile, today, you'd forget coats and colds and you'd
Follow the young people to morning Bible classes this week of camp,
Wipe the perspiration away after your game of volleyball,
Enjoy a refreshing swim in the river before supper,
Sit around the campfire tonight and hear Gospel tunes,
Pray in English as the Gospel is preached in Spanish, now that it's mid-summer in Chile.
It made a difference being in the U.S. this year because it:
United me with loved ones after six years' absence,
Brought hours of enjoyment with old friends and new-found ones,
Opened doors of witness in many parts of the country,
Provided physical rest and change (and added pounds!).
Brought heaps of memories to treasure and share when back in Chile for the next six years. (Unless He comes sooner.)
Your prayers will make a difference as you ask for:
Power of the Holy Spirit granted me to witness en route to Chile, Chilean Customs officers not to demand exorbitant duty on baggage,
A rapid adjustment made as I resumed third term duties in Chile,
A spiritual awakening at the Youth Convention Easter Week,
Our 25 Christian grammar schools and teachers as school year begins in March,
Those doing follow-ups with summer campaign converts,
The Bible Institute in Temuco and young people training there,
Permits to be granted Mr. Strong to continue

preaching to the military.

What a difference our Lord Jesus makes in all of life! Going back to Chile
is:

> Not a duty, to be faced unflinchingly. It's a privilege!
> Nor a way of wiping out the debt I owe Him for dying for me.
> I never could repay that debt.
> Not the result of pity for Chileans. They neither want nor
> need it.
> I go in love because He asks me to go, and
> Because He asks, I cannot stay.

And He is yours and mine, our Savior Jesus Christ,

> "Whom having not seen, ye love,
> In Whom, though now ye see Him not,
> Yet believing, ye rejoice
> With joy unspeakable and full of glory." (I Peter 1:8).

Thank you for your gifts, letters, cards, prayers and every
kindness.

Yours in Him Whose love never fades,

Consider a unique format or "trademark" which will immediately
identify you and add local color to your letter. One missionary from
Argentina draws an outline of mountains with a llama in the foreground
on all her letters. The Staffords make a pun on their name with a musical
score and the title "Staff Notes."

Many missionaries have adopted a newspaper style in their letters,
with columns and headings such as "Korhogo Klippings." As you can see
the format fosters a more brisk handling of the subject:

Korhogo Klippings

June, 19___

Melba Means — — B. P. 9, Korhogo, Republique de Cote d'Ivoire, West Africa

TYEBARA MARK READY

Senari-speaking Senufos of the north-ernmost tribe in the Ivory Coast are reading the Gospel of Mark in the Tyebara dialect this week. This is the first portion of the Word of God to be translated for them.

Many years of labor on the language have been necessary before the translation of Mark was possible. The grammar had to be analyzed and the language re-duced to writing. Many months have been spent in the translation and pro-duction of the manuscript.

As the last stencils were being typed last week the mimeograph machine broke down. It seemed that the actual produc-tion would be delayed several more weeks. Instead of the machine having to be sent 500 miles to Abidjan as ex-pected, Missionary Harold van den Berg was able to make the necessary repairs.

PINJA-ITES SEE PICTURES

Joyce Hornberger and Melba Means re-turned to Pinja to spend several days before Hornberger's departure for fur-lough. In January while visiting there for two weeks, they promised to return and show the pictures they were taking. With the kerosene projector and to the delight and amazement of the villagers, the Pinja-ites saw pictures of them-selves.

One young man, a house builder, heard that his picture had been shown in his absence. He breathlessly told Melba to wait and he would be right back to see the pictures--and how he did return!--dressed in his finest flooooowing white robe.

During the meeting, Tyelurugo, a former Moslem, confessed before fellow-villagers that she was walking the Jesus road during this visit by the

Look over your last prayer letter as you think about these seven questions:

1. Did it seem crowded or open?
2. Was it easy or hard to read?
3. Did I alter the form to accentuate the content?
4. Did I use drawings or photographs?
5. Would my prayer partners instantly recognize my letter because of a distinguishing feature?
6. Did I take advantage of available tools and materials, such as the decorative devices on my typewriter, colored paper, or colored ink?
7. Did the nature of my subject justify the length of my letter?

Try using these questions to improve the next prayer letter you write to your readers and prayer partners.

4

Many missionaries are nonplussed as to what to write about or if they should write at all during furlough. Imagine for a moment a coach who pulls his team off the field during the game. The team will not be able to score any points. The missionary who pulls his letters off the mission field also stands to lose. The answer is plain: if you want your prayer and financial support to continue, you must write regularly.

Furlough affords missionaries the opportunity to write from a unique perspective. You may reflect on your work from a distance after several months' absence. A letter of this nature will greatly benefit you as well as your reader.

Offer Fresh Insights

You may offer fresh insights into the religious and cultural life of your homeland. Cast your comments in positive rather than negative terms; describe your feelings and the adjustments you've made rather than attack the people or the churches you've visited.

Don't bore the reader with "housekeeping details," which contribute little to their overall understanding of missions. Don't write an inventory of everything you've done, such as what day you attended which meeting at camp or what weekend you visited which church.

Furlough letters should be warm and full of appreciation for your supporters at home. Note how one missionary built additional prayer support for herself and her adopted land. Her letter also gives the reader an "inside view" of a missionary and the purpose of furlough.

How does it feel to be home on furlough?
HOW DO I ANSWER THAT ONE? So many have asked it. So many

thoughts come to me about it — BUT —

How can I express my appreciation and ineffectiveness while talking to a housewife who prays and works in a kitchen paneled with missionary pictures and maps? Can I explain the warmth infilling me when I hear a Christian whom I have never seen before say, "I've been praying for you?" Can I measure the pleasure of knowing every letter received for five years was kept and the prayer requests remembered? Can I be thankful enough for the pure faith of a little child who kneels with the family and prays for the missionary as though she were a life-long friend? I cannot describe it — BUT — I sense it. It is as though a prayer canopy were covering me, and I praise God for the intercession IN BEHALF OF my ZAIRE.

Perhaps the answer is better explained by sharing the sight of a concerned father stepping forth from a congregation to declare, "Two of those young people who stood this morning were my children. I rededicated my own life to give them back to God. I'll help all I can to get them out on the field."

Or glimpse with me the radiance on the freckled-face youth of 17, dedicated for God's service on an ordinary Sunday evening. He is not yet conscious of the loneliness and monotony of real missionary life; but he is filled with the marvel of being called to preach. Such dedication is not just furlough fever and feelings. It is the whole spirit of missions. Once more we are compelled to praise him who calls FOR ZAIRE.

Sometimes the answer is more than feeling and seeing; more than prayer and dedication. It is the give and take — the sharing with the man behind the lines. He may be the pastor who declares, "I would have gone but God closed the door, so I'll stay and work for you here." He may be one of the administrative officials who plans the publicity, handles the money of the society, and shares in the task of arousing sleepy Christians. Behind the lines, too, are the girls in the office who work overtime hours on literature and letters or problems and principles. And all serve to remind me that I am just one small nut in the works as we labor for CHRIST IN ZAIRE.

Everyone knows the gloomier side of furlough feelings too. There is the constant circle of buses, trains, cars, meetings, conferences, and always one more step with a loaded suitcase. Add to that the pressure of schedules, the inadequacy of letters to keep in touch with the field, the loneliness in goodbyes and always the heart-cry to GET BACK TO ZAIRE!

YES, THIS IS BEING HOME ON FURLOUGH! All the praise and pain —the fruitfulness and frailty — the sacrifice and sharing — all of that YOU and ME feeling rolled into one reaction. With it all, I find myself praying, "They're behind me, Lord. They're praying me through. So help me, Lord, not to be impatient. Keep them faithful as I falter and learn of Thee. But, send me back, Lord. Send me quickly. Furlough feels fine, BUT ZAIRE IS WAITING."

Generate Follow-Up Prayer

The impact of a furlough letter can be far reaching. Consider the prayers and the funds that this missionary's letter will continue to generate after she leaves for the mission field:

Dear One who prays,

As I lay awake the other night for a long while in the moonlight I pondered the problem of outfit.

You see, I am within three months or so of packing, final medical exams, visa application and gangplank-climbing. Here among my things on the table in my room at the mission home is the note from the Chicago office: "We have a sailing date for you. Is June 29 on the Pacific Bear all right?"

List of Things NOT to Be Taken
1. Time clock--too rigid a schedule
2. Extroversion--lead in shoes which make visitation hard, the inner shrinking when someone calls at the door
3. Fear--of the "battlefront," of the future, of the tangle of group-relationships, of the Community shadow
4. Laziness
5. The loneliness of Jn 12:24
6. An unruly, untamed "member"--what havoc it works.

--and lots more--

The things to go into the trunk I listed long ago, and my family of churches are all helping in ways super-abundant: a rose-colored blanket, sheets, Bible study books. . . The boys' and girls' club in Oak Park, Ill., has been especially at work.

Norman and Evelyn Kendall, sponsors of the club, said to me once, "We notice you never give the club's name in your letters." My problem, I told them, was to have space to explain--for the club's name is the "Beabouts." There are about 40 of them, with Luke 2:49 for their motto and theme song--"Wist ye not that I must be about my Father's business?"

They are a lively bunch, and one of the features of each Sunday evening's meeting is a cash register around which they gather in gloriously orderly disorder to give their offerings for this missionary to Japan. I introduce them to you now, for those of you who get personal copies of these prayer letters get them via the folding, stamping, and mailing efforts of this club. Since September their offerings have gone for items for me to take back to Japan. Talk about being blessed!

As I finish the coming three months at Columbia University, I'm seeking to put into my things-to-take-back as much as I can of knowing Japan and the Japanese. There's something else, though. One of our missionaries, preparing for furlough, wrote of "things to be thrown away" and "souvenirs" and "things to be sorted." I did some sorting the night I lay awake--and came up with some things I want to be sure not to take back with me and things I must have, no matter how stiff the price. These things you can help me with--by prayer. Will you?

Outfit List

Things Imperative Regardless of Cost
1. Faith--deep-down conviction in every circumstance that my Father is in control
2. Love--with gentleness; easy to be intreated
3. Availability--like the missionary in Tibet who wanted never to be unavailable to the people
4. Humility--to serve, not to even miss not being served
5. Abiding--based on a will like Christ's: instantly, completely obedient to the Father

--and so much more--

Sincerely,

5

POSTSCRIPT

Missionaries **can** exert influence on the perceptions of the Christian public and especially on pastors and mission-minded people in the local church. The letters you write may be the only contact your readers have with the missions.

Your letters are the vital link between you and your readers, whether they are sent from the field or the furlough base. They affect the total missionary enterprise almost as much as the work you are doing on the mission field. Insofar as your letters multiply the number of new missionaries and stalwart prayer partners, they are as important as the meetings you conduct, the classes you teach, and the witnessing you do.

The cost to you in hard work and spiritual discipline is small compared to the eternal value of letters that are prayerfully and skillfully written.

APPENDIX A

Ten Commandments of Good Writing

1. Keep words, sentences and paragraphs short. Sentences should vary in structure and length. They should not exceed 20 words and should average 12 words.

2. Prefer the simple to the complex.

3. Use familiar words.

4. Avoid unnecessary words — cut ruthlessly as if you were an editor.

5. Use active not passive verbs.

6. Write the way you talk.

7. Tie your letters to your reader's experience. Proceed from the known to the unknown.

8. Use concrete words your reader can visualize. Abstract words dull your writing.

9. Add variety. Develop your own personal style.

10. Write to express — not to impress.

APPENDIX B

Rudolph Flesch has written several books on the art of writing. In his book, *The Art of Readable Writing* (Harper and Brothers, New York), he outlines a simple test which any writer can use in determining the "reading ease" of any piece of writing.

Why not take your last missionary letter and apply the two tests listed below?

1. Determine your "reading ease" score:
   Multiply the average sentence length (words)
   by 1.015   _____

   Multiply the number of syllables per 100 words
   by .846   _____

                                               Total _____

   Subtract this total from 206.835.   _____

   Your "reading ease" score is   Total _____

2. Determine your "human interest" score:

   Multiply the number of personal words per
   100 words by 3.635. (This includes pronouns,
   names of people, identifying names, generic
   terms such as folks, crowd, student, etc.)   _____

   Multiply the number of personal sentences per
   100 sentences by .314. (This includes direct
   statements to reader, quotations, questions,

command, exclamation, incomplete or frag-
mentary sentences)   _____

Your "human interest" score is: Total _____

Perfect score in both instances is 100.

Another increasingly popular formula for measuring the readability of
your writing is that of Robert Gunning, commonly known as the Fog
Index.

1. Count sample of 100 words.

2. Count number of difficult words (three or more syllables).

3. Compute average number of words per sentence.

4. Add answer for (2) to the answer for (3). Multiply the sum by the
    constant .4 (point 4). Your answer is approximate grade-in-school
    reading level.

Readers Digest has a Fog Index of 8; *Time,* 10; even the *Atlantic Monthly,*
commonly considered a highbrow magazine, has a Fog Index of 12 (high-
school senior level). If you really want to communicate with your home
constituency, probably your prayer letter should not have a Fog Index
rating of more than 10.

MY RECORD OF
Missionary Letters Sent Home

Date   Comments

MY RECORD OF

Missionary Letters Sent Home

Date   Comments

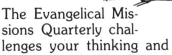

MEDIA ASSOCIATES INTERNATIONAL, INC.

(incorporating Evangelical Literature Overseas)

Media Associates International, Inc. (MAI) came into being in May 1985. It was born out of concern for national and mission leaders struggling with media ministries because of limited skills development and training. In 1986 Evangelical Literature Overseas (ELO) asked MAI to take over ELO's program. Through a merger in 1987 ELO became a part of MAI's global ministry.

MAI's purpose is to serve the worldwide Christian church and its mission and other agencies, in training personnel to become skilled communicators of the Gospel through the printed page and other media.

MAI is a not-for-profit publicly supported Christian agency and a member of EFMA/IFMA and also the Evangelical Council of Financial Accountability.

For further information please write or telephone:

Media Associates International, Inc.
Box 218
Bloomingdale, Illinois 60108-0218, USA
Telephone: (312) 893-1977